T0303203

PRAYING NAKED

The Journal Charles B. Wheeler Poetry Prize

PRAYING NAKED

KATIE CONDON

MAD CREEK BOOKS, AN IMPRINT OF
THE OHIO STATE UNIVERSITY PRESS
COLUMBUS

Published by Mad Creek Books, an imprint of The Ohio State University Press.

Library of Congress Cataloging-in-Publication Data is available online at catalog.loc.gov.

Cover design by Angela Moody
Cover art by Dorielle Caimi, *Until Proven Innocent*
Text design by Juliet Williams
Type set in Palatino Linotype

♾ The paper used in this publication meets the minimum requirements of the American National Standard for Information Sciences—Permanence of Paper for Printed Library Materials. ANSI Z39.48–1992.

For my parents
with eternal gratitude

Contents

Origin

I was born inside a mourning dove.
There is wind in all of us.

Here I am
in a century that has its eyes

shut tight—don't I know exactly
why I'm here. In the end

the sun varnishes us all
in amber. Undress

for that light. There is flight
in all of us. Find me

in the pasture sewing
bluebonnets into each bend

of our laughter. I was born
inside the decayed mourning

dove you found shaded
in lavender. Call me *maggot.*

When you die, don't worry.
I will rise up from you

opaque as the angel
admiring your rotted waist.

I, too, will die—am
dying—though I

am a maggot, though I covet
fragrance from your breathless

flowering. I am born
from grieving. I am

as afraid as you.

On the seventh day God says, *What you've got is virgin charm & a knife in your pocket.*

& I'm like, *Thanks?*

The heart finds its anchor in the sky.

The woman is told she is a tabernacle.

On the forty-third day, I confuse my hangover for grief.

God says, *Your longing will be for me, & I will dominate you.*

& I'm like, *Nope!*

The morning wears a cotton dress.

Is this all I will amount to:

> The hot breath of months in my pocket?
> Every telephone pole I mistook for a tree?
> The melancholy suspicion of library security?

Nah.

The bartender hums the tune
of a hummingbird rising from its flower.

I say, *I inherited Sappho's pussy*
& I believe me.

God says, *Thou shalt not kill.*
& I'm like, *But what about with my eyes.*

I never asked for the capacity to love
ugly things, but here I am.

Carnation, daisy, lavender lately the lavender of late.

I boil my stock exclusively with wishbones.

I say, *I like my men smooth & far away, reticent*
as a bookshelf.

& God butts in, *I can do that for you.*

His eyes search me like a pendulum.

I've scraped a dead man's ashes out
from under my fingernails like lice eggs.

A woman raised in contest with other women is a child of God.

God says, *This is getting serious.*
& I'm like, *You bet.*

I remember my ignorance
& miss it.

The skies open silently with a woman's legs.

Morning glory, morning glory, morning hallelujah.

The Sacrifice's Prayer

I cannot offer you a sky & an egret
or a small marsh & thirty turtles
gathered & sunning all in a row.

You are not an airboat—not a steeple
from which I hang my white sails.
Perhaps you are a window, or a vessel

tailored for the soul & the quiet
tinks of rain on a car-hood—for my voice
that said, *I grabbed the blanket from the bed*

of my truck, when I really wanted
to grab the rain & sea. There is a sea
at the back of my eyes.

In it, a dock & your body bobbing
in waves disjointed by wind.
You are not a house, not a journey.

The hand with which I bless you
knows no God—is not so proud
to prevent me from falling to my knees

& huddling there with childless
murmuring. Your pity like the dark
lull of the marsh.

The shipping channel is dredged
& deep, dredged & deep.
I've seen you gather the sea

around your face like a mask.
Help me mask me. I cannot find mine.
It is somewhere here—

I've felt its sleep for years
beating its fists against
the dark in my eyes.

Aubade

There are mornings that don't breathe at all.
Always arriving, the jays appear. Or
the morning exhales and I nod at the sun.
I take my birth control right on time.

Imagine: the glare of so many windshields
made of rain; dawn's abandoned husk on the lawn.
Listen to me! I plead to no one. Right now, if I were a
mother, darkness would wait—or come running.

My own mother said this:
If a woman held her infant by the feet from a window,
I'd understand.

In the air-dew, hummingbirds battle over sugar water.
This is a symbol for my life. I fight and fight. I wake up.
Steam rises, then disappears, above a dark stream.
The mist a swaddle for no thing.

Praying Naked

I've never let a man love me
without feeling very Mary Magdalene about it.

Just the other night I was dancing with a friend
of a friend & he got handsy & I got servant-minded,

letting him move his grip from my waist to my hips
& lower, while a Motown bass boomed through the opaque

& sweaty darkness. It wasn't guilt I felt
when I decided I was obliged to let him

explore the finer points of my swaying
body. Maybe it was loneliness. Maybe

it was my own desire to be desired, since, if a man
wants me, I know I have at least a little worth left.

Or it's payback for the hours I spent treating
every bead on the rosary as the Virgin Mary's nipples,

pressing each one to my mouth
& murmuring her own prayer over them.

If I have offended the Lord
in my manner of worship, then the Lord

should not have made women so beautiful.
Look at us. Even when we are stripped

of our bodies—reduced to prayers & beads, shadows
the music rubs its hum against—even then

we are gorgeous. & even then we are unsure

of our worth. Lord, if you will not let me exist
without shame at least leave me while I whisper

over my blessed mother's naked body
the words you said would save me.

My mother gives a man permission

to slit her throat. The incision
no larger than a vulva's inner lips,
the surgeon slips his slender tools in.

It is simpler than her first time,
he says—the nodules curled in the throat
almost at peace.

Rain, & in the late morning
my knees scraped from kneeling
at the mouth of the lake.

Simpler, but not the last time,
he says—death growing again
& again because it grew

the first time. My first lover
forever dressing in my car's backseat
by the lake. In her neck,

death's conception like a hand
curling to a fist. In the hospital,
my mother willing birth

& so I was. In the hospital,
some man willing life
& so she is, still.

Death curls & hardens, rain
gaining speed, rising
heat in the backseat

& I was—am—far
from the edge of forgiving
my mother for giving me

a body. Gaining speed, she
wakes, sewn. Rain, late
morning, shore

so familiar it bleeds.

Volatile Elegy

I left a very convincing suicide note in the chrysanthemums.
How I love pollen & my sticky fingers!

Is being dead all fun & games?
This comet will sleep upon this park bench.

In my hair, tangled like the possibility of life elsewhere,
God places a flower.

3 a.m. & the North Star writhing. A mourning dove. A glassy eye.
The stars are what the dead get hard for.

Sometimes I love god, & sometimes I love geraniums.
Take it, the sorrow my mouth makes.

A flower for the lady who is so beautiful.
A lady for the ground that is so beautiful.

I hold my lust like a pool in my palm
(some honey for the dead) (some nectar for my God).

Tonight the stars will share my bed.

What Matters Most

The pines; the moan   trains cleave   through the night with;
    my father   hardening   against porn   he'll forget
to delete   from the browser history   while the creek
    hurries down   a cliff face   & my mother leans
against her window   to hear that water's   pulsing;   white
  powder from a moth   wing left on   the porch light
I sit beneath   watching the sage   I grew from seed
    observe its home   above the parking lot   while a spider builds
(as my mother did)   a home   where it can manage one.
Tell me   that the mountains   reignite, that snow
    gasps itself back   into air,   that the plane
flying overhead   carries people   who want
              to arrive where they land—   that the night
    will rupture   into a morning   heavy
with rain   & fledglings.   I am not convinced
              that my desire   to sing
    to the lake   I want to lose   my breath in
matters in the slightest   —but that   foothill   &
    the tractor-trailer   heaving itself up it   that cicada   this
horizon gray   with downtown's insistent   light   my breath still

insisting   its presence in   my chest   like a hymn   like a

hymn sung   to oneself   in the car   after years

it bursts from   the pew shelf   into my hands

the dust that   follows   matters   it settles

in the outstretched   hands   of the light.

Hymn

Standing on the deck mid-rain
I watch the wind rouse the pines,

their needles brittle
& thirsty. Earlier, the professor

with three degrees demanded I say
"phallus" instead of "penis"

in our discussion of *Othello*
& I know I'm being obvious

when I say these pines are phallic,
that they could be God's

dick pressing hard into the earth
some believe he continues to make new

but I've already said it—forgive me.
Dear God, this is not a prayer:

penis dick cock balls

The pines are writhing.

penis dick cock balls

What good is the wind, what good
is my mouth, if I am only allowed
to name politely?

Even God shouts
Penis dick cock balls!

The rain falls all over his face
& you can't tell him that isn't
happiness.

God, your silhouette is smooth
& slender on the curtains.

penis dick cock balls

Dear God, come to bed
while rain slips through the sky's sieve

& the birds flit around that wetness
like tongues.

penis dick cock balls

This is not a prayer.

This is wind, this is pine
bending breathless

into the wetness night sheds.

penis dick cock balls
penis dick cock balls

My voice, a little
God crudely sculpted.

Katie Condon, an American, One of the Roughs, a Kosmos in the Flesh.

You have never touched a woman if you haven't touched me.

I call to you from where I swim near the shore. When I call to you, my breasts rise from the water so nicely.

Not even you can resist me. There is not a single gray hair on my

soul. Hot soul! Soul of
sweat & lipstick, soul positioned
in truth! Soul cloaked

by my bright body rising now from the river's clutch. My soul calling you. My breasts & heart & hips sidling up in the grass to meet you.

Feel even my cheek against your palm.

Is it my clamor that stalls you? I shout at the sky & claw its ether down so you might lay me upon it.

When you take my body finally into your mouth, my soul will not return the love you offer me. I will not thank you for liking the touch of me.

I know it is good for you to do so.

We Need to Talk

It's not that I don't love you
or that I'm incapable of loving.

I don't know how to love only you.

Listen: I love you today
& also Bradley the busboy from the Bourbon Orleans Hotel Bar
who, when he collected my half-eaten po'boy, smirked at me
like I was a crawfish he'd love to clean out.

& yesterday I loved Jason,
the Swiss yoga instructor at LA Fitness,
whose voice lilts like a harp from the front of the room—
& I know you know that a voice is a jet on which I fly
first class into the arms of desire, but, honey,
know I loved you deeply yesterday, too.

I do wish love were simpler.
Like the birds & the bees.

Actually,
I know very little about how birds love.
But I know bees have fucked the roses into cliché.

You are cliché.
Or if you're not, you will be.

Darling, what man wouldn't I love to be a flower?

Ode to Gabriella

I buy larkspur on the one-week anniversary
of the musician not calling me back.

More than likely he's out with Gabriella, a violinist
he's been seeing according to a mutual friend.

I am no musician (never had the patience to practice)
but what I lack in patience I make up for in nerve:

Gabriella, you are beautiful.

When you pull your bow across his strings
your arms bend like my larkspur bends toward morning.

Your curls slide across your chest like glissandos
he'll sing while you compose yourself atop him.

Gabriella, lift your head up from that tired instrument.
I have lips full as hydrangeas. Your legs, each a stalk in bloom.

Bend yourself toward my morning
& let me climb into you like a bee into a foxglove.

Let's root ourselves on every highway median,
in every rancher's pasture. Come with me

my tall flower, my sweet Gabriella.
Fill my entire field with your overtures.

Timestamps

Ten hours ago, Adam Liddy liked my profile picture
alone in his Asheville apartment. My brown eyes coaxed him back
seven months to the time I pulled him by his shirtsleeve
onto the dance floor in the barn, poured him
a shot of bourbon, shared a blanket on the porch, asked him
to close the flue of the woodstove at the party
because it was getting too hot. He must've remembered
my laughter as I climbed onto the puny wooden raft
at midnight to listen to him describe what being suddenly
lusted after by many women feels like & how he would
never cheat on his girlfriend. *Never,* he said.

Nine hours ago, Adam Liddy wrote me an e-mail
to catch me up on his life: his non-existent & therefore perfect
teaching load, his new foreign fellowship, & his recent
breakup. What he didn't write but wanted to
was that he'd convinced himself desire isn't tangible
unless you act on it—that when we climbed into the trailer
storing the left-handed desks, that when I sat down in one
& looked up at him, just before a security guard
shined his flashlight onto my shadowed face,
desire wasn't thrashing around like a snake under his boot.

What I didn't say but should've was: *Adam,*
I'd never cheat on my boyfriend, either—& I wouldn't.
But there's nothing wrong with getting off on the shape tension takes in a small space,
with lifting your eyes up over the wall you've built & named *Life*
to see how you might be different.

Adam, there's nothing wrong with desiring what you know you can't have—
nothing wrong with playing with potential
like a house cat plays with a bird it won't mean to kill.

Giving Myself Advice

Katie, it's clear you want to tear through his body
like a derailed freight car through a turnip field.
Forgive me for sounding aggressive.
All I mean is recklessness turns you on.

Admit it, you love a lawless man:
a man who scales mountains without any underwear on,
a man who can open you up
a stubborn bottle of beer using only his teeth.

The art of recklessness is hard to get right—
it's about finesse, which might not make sense
to you lately, Katie. You, who scrolls through Facebook
all morning, thinking an act of recklessness

is sharing the cat video your mom posted
on your great aunt's wall, which you're watching now
for the third morning in a row!
Katie, get off your ass & be somebody

somebody would like to fuck.
This does not make you an object—it makes you
Desire itself! Desire, when you want
to lure a reckless man do not shout

that you're going to plow through his body
like a derailed freight car through a turnip field
(the poem began poorly). No, Desire, if you love
a reckless man, do not chase him on his tiny misadventures.

Let him scale you like a cliff face
only after he's chased you down your tracks
for a good while, eyes wide & mouth open,
gathering what he can of your madly showering sparks.

At Poetry Readings I'm Always Drunk

I put on lipstick & ride my bike to the reading for the erotic juxtaposition.

I have conversations & pretend I smoke cigarettes by smoking them.

I rise from my chair with Holly Golightly–type laughter & grace

& I hope I am being sexualized by everyone.

I knock back a shot & sit somewhat still listening to people read

like capital-P-poets & buy their books mostly out of confusion.

Sometimes, the poems aren't afraid of mystery

& people get dense with quiet.

On coasters, I write down the lines I'm convinced I'll reuse later, like:

I write to be historically alone.

To the readers, I speak ineptly about how happy I am

to have met them. How honestly I want to live

& not too quickly. From the other side of the big room,

I watch myself mumble self-consciously. Smile

stupidly. In my mind, I'm already riding my bike into the old night,

like a drunk astronaut toward the moon.

I'm a Kick-Ass Woman

Ask anybody. This ass has never been kicked
to the curb. I do the kicking. I'm a nasty-ass woman
drinking chamomile tea at dusk. I know what I've got
& it's a throne for an ass. Grab it. Kiss it. Pop
the pimple on that ass. See what happens when you
disagree with my ass. I've got a bad-ass ass. A kick-ass ass.
A good-pair-of-jeans-is-hard-to-find–type ass. Cue Flannery's
ass, as broad & innocent as a cabbage. I'm getting literary
on your ass. Listen: you can't have *passion*
without *ass.* Or *Parnassus.* Make way for my poetic ass,
as essential & enduring as your thesaurus
but sexier. I'd tattoo the *Cantos* on my ass
if it would make it less boring. This Is Just to Say: *A Carafe Is a Blind*
Ass, or: I'm no Modernist. I'm the future
of The Poetics of Kick-Ass—the voice of a nation
from the mouth of a woman with the keys
to the van that fits all of your sweet asses. Climb in.
We're bound for the coast. Bet your ass
we'll be there before dawn. Sit back & watch
my Walt Whitman dashboard hula girl shake his ass
all the way across the American desert
we'll make an oasis of by the time we're through.

After All, Saint Catherine Is My Namesake

Because I have no food to give
I give the stray cat a quick scratch behind her ears
& now she won't stop mewing
for more on my windowsill. Her green
eyes are as wide as my own

the first time I moved aside
my panties for a boy: crowded in my car's backseat
I wore a red dress & smelled like the honey
of my mother's biblical heaven!

God, my mother lectured, *watches our every move*:
watched the boy indelicately take me into his mouth,
pretending he knew exactly what to do.

I'm pretending I don't hear that damn cat's *mew mew mew.*
Imagine if I'd lost my virginity mewing!

If anything I was bored,
waiting for God to tap on my windshield & praise me
for how selflessly I offered myself to the hungry.

When the professor asked the workshop, *Who among us now will speak about poetry ideologically*? I thought with abandon *ME!* & then

I googled "ideology" that night when I got home. Who am I
kidding? I know nothing about bodies of theory, though I read

as much Kant as I can. At the end of the day, all I can recall
is the way the light tripped down from the fluorescent bulbs

onto my mother's face when they wheeled her past us
into post-op. How the sutures they used to close the slit in her neck

looked less like lifelines than I assured myself they would. Teach me something
about the ideology of women: how we can crave motherhood

& autonomy at the same time, knowing both are gardens for loneliness
despite our daughters or our lovers leaving our face damp with reckless kissing.

I'm sure Freud has opinions about why daughters & lovers & mothers share
the same hotel room in my unconscious, but my intentions are pure: I want to
 learn

the path my mother's finger traveled down the sternum of the first person she
 fucked
but didn't love so I can grieve her not as a nation grieves its commander, but as a
 woman

grieves another woman. We all know we turn into our mothers, & hers died
 young
in the grip of her body's disease. Please, tell me one more time

what Derrida said about language—was it that we can deconstruct it
as we do a cadaver: cut into a word to understand

what prevented it from keeping itself alive? I don't know. I don't know
much beyond what language does when I fuss with it

& put it all in tidy rows—that a word can walk toward me then
like my mother's ghost. That it can be dusk all day. That we are self-taught

in the philosophy of our own desire. If I speak ideologically,
it's because I desperately want to know the exact stitch

memory & language used to weave each other into the dress
my mother picked out special, knowing how beautifully it'd fall to the floor.

In Winter

Even the deer love convenience.
Their droppings litter the grassy path to the tree line
dad plowed for mom so she can reach the compost pile
when business draws him away.

Twilight turns the snow blue & the trees
are cello strings the wind pulls its bow across.
Driving home after dinner, mom says
she wants a dog, but is feeling timid—lately,

when the opportunity of a companion presents itself
the bitch miscarriages, or the pup tests positive
for a fatal disorder, or my mom's own body gives out
(for the second, third, fourth time).

Adopting a dog isn't worth the risk, mom says,
the snow on the driveway left black from her spinning tires.
From the living room, I watch the deer
emerge from the woods as slow as twilight.

They bow their heads—as mom bows hers now
either into prayer or sleep—& they begin to eat
the waterlogged & shit-strewn grass.
So this is what it's like, coming home.

Mom snores herself awake,
straightens up, tends to her knitting.
On the path, the deer are little bass clefs.
The wind's enormous instrument urges us all into night.

At the #1 Fried Chicken & Seafood

Before I knew what *senza tema d'infamia ti rispondo* meant
I thought it meant *the angels from their perches descend*
like grackles to collect my soul & other souls.

Collected first will be my mother's soul, since she is so close to dying.
Senza tema d'infamia ti rispondo—I am twenty-five & far from dying
& walk with great purpose to the fried-chicken joint

where I speak with homeless men about my life openly.
Like angels from their perches, grackles fly down
to eat food people let fall from to-go boxes

& all of their eyes are black & small, so small.
Senza tema d'infamia ti rispondo.
Away with you, birds, who glare at me

like my dying mother!
My mother who has been dying
slowly since I was a little girl.

Ti rispondo, ti rispondo.

Outside of the restaurant, I always intend to speak
with homeless men briefly & of the weather only
but it never works out.

I hand them my name like a dollar:
Katie. Ti rispondo. Katie. Ti rispondo.
Katie,   Katie,   Katie.

Those homeless men clutch my name
against their chests like a dollar that will love them.
Senza tema & they grab my arm

senza tema & I run from them
like my mother runs from death: very slowly
despite her effort—

senza tema, ti rispondo,
death is coming,
it is coming.

Of death I intend always to speak bravely
& of strangers' deaths only
but it never works out.

I know *senza tema d'infamia ti rispondo* means
without fear of infamy I answer
but what does it mean

that my mother's dying, has been dying
has been has been has been?
Senza tema d'infamia ti rispondo:

I'm afraid like a grackle.
Like an angel.
Like a mother.

Senza tema d'infamia ti rispondo.

She is less afraid of dying
than she is of living.
Has been. Has been. Has been.

Senza tema. Ti rispondo.
Death is coming.
There it goes.

Don't Be Bitter, Baby!

"Each one of my breasts," she cried, "is 3 lbs
of pure gold
& if you don't believe me, tough!"

She thinks the secret to possessing
beauty is to be nauseously overwrought about everything

& I hate to admit, but occasionally she's right:

sometimes the only way to solve my hunger is to scream
I have a vast lust for beef! as I drive through
McDonald's at 3 a.m.

& sometimes wearing a boa to the supermarket
is the only cure for my sorrow.

She tells me I glitter
& brags that the guy she took home last night
looked like the love child of George Clooney & God.

The world isn't ugly, she tells me, if you let it borrow your stilettos.
She giggles, "Don't be bitter.
Eat lipstick. Sob onto your mirror."

& I do,

each tear ballooning the reflection of my grievances
falling red from my hypocritical mouth.

Parable

Rage & oregano. The open window. The lawn.

A fledgling hops the nest
while the robin is gone.

Steam from the pot.
Tomatoes. Tomatillos. Ricotta.

Same as anywhere else: a mother's corpse stored

in an armoire of ash. There is want

for miracle. Aspen shade. Chrysanthemums.

Caterpillar in the basil Mother said
you should have killed.

Liver & current. Blood & sand. Dove songs. Early kale.

Mother said,
Desire digs a pretty grave.

You balance on her tomb.
Foxglove. Forsythia. A bad spill
on the white carpet.
Get the bleach. Hold

the baby.

The fledgling shakes in the cardboard box.

Dusk bears dawn bears dusk.

Driving, 4 a.m.

As if the valley were a wound, fog
covers it with its gauze, rendering the light
worthless, so I pull the car over and sob.

Somewhere in these mountains there is a robin
watching her nest from a neighboring pine
and somewhere there is a falcon screeching

for its mate and somewhere in another life
I am not on the side of the road wishing the doe
crossed the highway a few moments sooner

so I'd have a reason to lift myself out of myself
and drift over to inspect the intestines that tumbled out
of the gash my Toyota ripped in her belly.

It's been so long since I've understood the world
as a place I deserve to be alive in. Somewhere beyond
this valley, people I love are long ago asleep

and when they wake they will know only as much
of me as I let them. How easy I've made living seem.
How willingly the mountains lent me their flaking

birch and bird song, their rising mist and moss
so I could mask my constant hum of pain
and enter each day convincingly alive.

Wherever there is beauty there is intention
to grow numb in it. Somewhere in another life
I am already dead and somewhere in the mountains

there is a black bear gliding across a ridge
glaring down at the valley where I remain wary
of the stretch of road I cannot see.

How to Know the Wildflowers

On YouPorn there is a girl getting fucked
in a field filled with wildflowers.

She doesn't moan like the other porn stars
screwed from behind by plumbers & pool boys.

Quiet in my computer's blue glow, she delivers
her body, bending willingly to his whims.

If she is the wind, he is a quavering thistle,
his thorns reaching out to cut her breasts

for no good reason. This is not the first time
I am drunk & crying watching free porn.

I touch my breast like that will remove his thorns.
Is it wrong to feel a hurt kind of beautiful?

Buckwheat. Honeysuckle. Swamp-rose-mallow.

Poem from the Mouth of God

There is a reason
I have yet to let anyone
see my face. I am a lonely man

& socially inept. I send angels
into women's rooms
because I never mastered the art

of non-offensive pickup lines
& even with a wingman
only one woman's ever said yes.

She is tired of me.
Who can blame her
when I spend my days

at every window in the house
shuttering & unshuttering myself
from the view I created

& grew afraid of? My son
doesn't visit anymore
& you're not surprised.

Me neither. After centuries,
the first miracle I performed
was this morning

when I raised myself
out of bed & lifted a razor
to my horrible face.

What advice do I have left,
except that you should make things
& keep them closer to you than ethers away?

Do not be like me.
This light is the only good
I've offered you,

but even light, too often, dies
in a furious burst.

Getting Through Monday

It's difficult lately to see the point
in even the world's most beautiful efforts.

For instance, the fog that covered the creek this morning
like a veil the wind moved aside every so often
so the light could soften the water's rough face

or the little blonde girl who sang
My Darling Clementine to the monarch butterfly
she cradled dead in her hands.

Today, even the prospect of making
love is unfulfilling. The sun is out
& I have no reason to be dismal.
I don't want to die.

I have so far understood my life
as something I can control,
realize now it is not, & for recognizing this
many say I should be grateful.

I'm working on it.

In the meantime, life slogs through me
like a slug through the garden & other people die
for no good reason while I watch construction workers
move across the roof they're building
& consider how this scene could stand for time—

how each shingle is a year in our lives & each nail
something beautiful passing through it,
anchoring us to the scaffolding (which is memory)
& reminding us that we have no choice
but to be here until the rain
soaks us weary & we fall, leaving only
dust (which is the soul) & heaps of concrete.

Vow

On nights I can hear the owl calling from the woods,
the moon is no longer the only thing I project myself onto

& thank God because if Sarah says *ampersands are so 2009*
then I can only imagine what year the moon went out of style.

I wonder if Sappho knew when she wrote,
"gem light / not one human heart has ever resisted it

or the moon," that one day the moon would be a faux pas?
That owl is Sappho & Sarah can be the moon

& I will remain my same self alone in bed wondering
if what I'm hearing now is the wind or a gentle rain beginning

& here is Sappho calling me from the woods, saying
Come with me, Katie, & Don't bother with your clothes,

& I won't—I will let Sarah's old light dress me
& if it is raining the rain will adorn me like 3,000 sapphires

she will consider long out of vogue, forgetting
that time & its made-up constraints don't concern me,

especially since I am near the edge of the woods now,
the place where time cannot follow.

I promise you this:
even if my words are destroyed they will be remembered.

The Real Self Is Very Scary

Last night I woke up from a great sex dream
that wasn't a dream at all. I was scared of myself,
for even when I was unconscious I was willing.

The real self is very scary is a line I stole from a poet
who, I'd bet anything, has also been awakened
by her lover in the middle of the night, half aroused
& half terrified because she wasn't in control.

But when am I in control?

Half the time I am dreaming of my students
sprouting a second set of arms & wrapping them around me—
of their being so strong they carry me without a struggle
down the hall to the principal's office, where I am reprimanded
for showing them a poem about human grief.
Half the time I am clawing my way out of a dream
about my mother growing flowers
from her chest so she'll look *pretty in her casket,*
& her hair falls out by the handful.

I don't know if there is a God
despite my mother trying to convince me of him for nearly 30 years.
If there is a God, then I've definitely never been in control.

Or have I—

I am thinking of certain men who I have awakened
& stolen from their static lives. Of men I've laid down in groves
of poison ivy & pleased under the moon, which was cliché
until just now when I reclaimed the moon.
Moon, you have seen me control the hands of men, have you not?
These men, who I have let have me.
To whom I have said, *the real self is very scary.*
& I wasn't lying, was I.

To Every Woman Who's Been Kept a Secret

I'm talking about you, Laurel.
About Saturday night when it took your boyfriend
five hours & six beers to bring you up.

Laurel, I don't know where you are, but at the bar
your name spilled from his mouth like moonlight across the creek
I initially hoped he & I'd wade naked into.

What else could I do but think of you somewhere in this same night
laughing, maybe dancing, and as unaware as I was
that the other of us existed. The worst part, Laurel,

is I can't bring myself to blame him—
it's easy to say secrecy is bred by lust, but believe me
lust has little to do with it.

We're all bored, Laurel. I am, aren't you?

On Saturday night, your boyfriend kept you secret
so I could be a pawn he moved
across his board of "In Another Life."

In his other life, Laurel, you are a nun in love with Brad Pitt,
& I am the fountain the penny's thrown into, & he is a bachelor
with a bottle of bourbon and a waterbed.

In another life, he is smoking cigars on a yacht in Shanghai.
Or he is a lion eluding his hunter. Or he is Lenny Kravitz
feeling sexy, if lonely, in his leather. He wants to be the falcon

at rest in the cedar. He wants to be the falconer
alone in the field. He wants to believe he is a martyr
in his real life—that we are the hay the fire flares up from.

And so what if we are? Laurel, so what if we're the flame
that makes him scream? I say it's all to the good. Let him burn
with the whole world watching. It's what he doesn't know

he wants—to be worthy of something fiercer than he is.
Of a woman's fire. Of the affection we have for him
even as we reach up and wrap his bones in our heat.

To the woman who accused me of not being a feminist, I'm sorry

for pointing out that we are subject to
& act upon the same ugly desires

that fuel the men who've used us.
I apologize for every time I've confessed

I need a man's love, & meant it.
Forgive me, please, for continuing

to believe that roses are beautiful.
Pardon me for loving them more as they wilt,

heavy with dreams of being scattered
down wedding aisles. It's true:

the mornings I'm coated in sweat & come
& hear the train heaving over the river

past smoke stacks pushing up their innards
I don't pause to consider how the world is home

to a million angry phalluses.
Can you blame me? Look at my man

lying there soaked in what light makes
it through the curtains—his thin

& gorgeous mouth slack & silenced
by pleasure our body afforded him.

You can't tell me women should be ashamed
of their impulse to please—

that we should cast each breast in iron
& march into the day daring it to try & love us.

I am not sorry I mirror the desire
none of us can fend off.

If you insist, I will leave you
to your heavy-breasted troops

& climb back into bed
where I'll resume my life's work.

Argument for Loving from a Distance

Raining this morning and the foothills are dusted
with the gray light that comes with bad weather.

Even through the water's falling sound
the train makes itself heard across the city

like church bells at midnight. What beautiful moaning
loudness becomes when it's forced to stretch itself

across a distance. Like the way my lover's song greets me
from upstairs, where he's singing in my shower—

even across our short reach, his voice sounds truer
than it does when he sings and I am near him. Listening

to him croon through the water's heavy moving,
I'm certain Eurydice was pleased

when Orpheus looked back too soon.
How happy it is to die twice

when your reward is your lover's real voice
reaching you across wind and water and time.

How relieving the realization he is more himself
without you than when you are spread out

naked below him, your hair tangled in his palms
and his song diluted from your sating his longing.

What is constant across all love
is the inevitability of its end.

One of us will grow bored
or one of us will die and, knowing this,

Eurydice was best to leave love early.
Wait too long and he'll stop

singing, even from a distance. Go
now! Run from your love! May your absent

touch be the bells he hears clanging out from the steeple
into the gray night that slows into morning,

where the train will try to out-moan the wind,
where he will liken this moaning to the way

you sounded beneath him. He will pick up his lust
like a lyre and sing your name trying to reach you

wherever you are. And wherever you are
you will hear his song haunting the air like mist.

Listen to how entirely he loves you, for the first time.

To an Ex-Lover's Daughter

At the quarry, where your father
fucked me the first time, campfire ash
coated the flowers.
                                        I am vain

and bottle my grief like perfume.
The fifth time we fucked, your father whispered
things like:
                    On the trail today I stopped
            by the birches and the birches
                        told me [something about love].

My cherry blossom perfume scented
your mother's
                    divorce papers. When you seek

me out and ask, *Why?*
I don't know what I'll say.
What can I offer but a mirror
                                        you might learn from:

I don't believe myself worthy
of merciful men.

Don't dress yourself in that ash.

Desire Is a Sickness

Outside of the Super Gas in Cookeville, TN,
some guy in a Yankees hat says: *the trees are going apeshit,*
which means their leaves are red now and falling

but I don't notice them much. Instead
I'm thinking of the woman who wrote
Amber Asan of Nashville is a homewreking whore

on the station's bathroom wall and I'm thinking
of Amber, too—whether either of them
is still in Nashville or cares about that man

they passed between them without knowing
which woman he wanted most. Near the pumps,
a little girl catches a leaf spinning from a maple

and says something about fire that I barely hear.
I've been called a home-wrecker
for welcoming Desire when it strut in
with a cigarette in one hand and an agenda in the other.

I've had the stupid thought
that men were meant to be with me
because they said so and because the sun

was hitting their faces through the trees
in such a way their skin was covered
in tiny seas of light. At the pump behind me

an SUV plays an impossible love song.
The trees drop more of their leaves—their
emboldened nakedness a ritual
that families park to watch.

Desire is a sickness we all want.

From Space, the Wildflowers Are One Bouquet on the Valley's Grave

In lieu of flowers, I collected amber
sap for my mother from the dying
tree. From space, she purred,

That tree is dying and you
are taking away what it created
to heal. It was a flowering tree.

Invisible from space, the lightning
loved it too hard. Remember
that one time I was beautiful

enough to be in a movie? I sat
yards away from a weeping
cherry. All that wind.

The married man pulled an orphaned
petal from my hair. His wife
the entire pasture of poppies

prepared for starlight.
She, a mother. Death
sticky in her hands, my mother

would not speak to me for days.
I was not a mother
yet. You could see that

from space. Was I
the lightning or the eye
of the satellite, blind

to everything but the valleys
wild and teeming with bees?
Either way, the wildflower

and all her mothers are accounted for
from space—every comet
a witness to their bloom.

Real Elegy

I will not write: *O! Voices of the ever-living*
tongue of earth, rejoice! I write the dead down

the way the ground wrote them down:
using the roots of many flowers.

Practicing Digressions

for Richard

I am eager to grow old. What a joy
it will be to bear love down
on whatever daughters I force

into this sometimes lovely world
preaching similar things, I bet,
that my mother preached to me

—like, *You are a woman. Praise*
yourself. What a light her scriptures are
on this morning that is gray and cool

as the last lake on the mountain
before it gives itself up to the sky.
I meant to be telling you about

age, not my mother, who is aging,
not mountains or mornings
or the unforgivingly expansive sky. I admit

it will be difficult not to mention
the robin on the wire, the light
lifting itself up over my husband's

slender body, which he lives in more
confidently than I have witnessed of myself.
I am practicing digressions on you

so that I can prepare for the ways my
memory will loosen itself from around
itself, uncoiling like the threads

in the ice-skating penguins sweater
I'll love when I'm eighty
and never want to take off, even

as summer's weight bears
down like my mother bore down
on me—my mother, whose voice

is familiar in this poem, though years
will have bounded by since I heard her
sing. Where was I—mountains, steep

as memory. Water, morning, light.
My husband's body stirring, his hands
trembling after thousands

of mornings exploring every new
wrinkle on my breasts. Have I
spoken of birds? How they stay

on longer into the cold than
they should, and for what? To learn
how to forage for food that is not there,

to harvest something finally of absence
that they will keep with them
when they decide to flit off

into the thick mist of late fall
that, when I was young, I wanted
to walk through, believing

I would make myself a ghost.

Resurrection

If a son can do it, so can a mother. Mine, even. Watch her
gallop through the airport, a giddydrunk dove, amazed
by her own mobility.

How appropriate her tomb
was made of her own body. How typical
of a mother. O, deadalive woman, you used a body
to make another body. This time, one all your own.

I was a skeptic. I wrote you dead & dead & dead
& yet you rose each morning, buoyant
with sun. Call me *Judaschild* who took the bag of coins
from the one who bet you eternally dead.

Have I sinned?

It was a relief to imagine you mortal
like me: your body a walking tremor, carting a haul
of cannibal cells. O, hunger & thirst. O, the evergrowth
of death in a mother & its arrival
& its halt.

Forgive me, Mother, if I have sinned.

Name me *doubtswaddled child,*
preemptive griefdaughter.

Today, through the airport, I walk
cast in your shadow, the velvet homedarkness

that created me.

Acknowledgments

Thank you to the editors and staff of the following journals where these poems, sometimes in earlier versions and with different titles, first appeared: *The Adroit Journal,* "The Sacrifice's Prayer" (originally titled "For the Christening of a Ship"); *Bloom,* "At Poetry Readings I'm Always Drunk"; *Blunderbuss,* "After All, St. Catherine Is My Namesake," "Volatile Elegy," "Don't Be Bitter, Baby!," and "How to Know the Wildflowers"; *BOAAT,* "On the seventh day God says, *What you've got is virgin charm and a knife in your pocket*"; *The Columbia Review,* "My Mother Gives a Man Permission"; *Copper Nickel,* "In Winter" and "Resurrection"; *Four Way Review,* "Argument for Loving from a Distance," "I'm a Kick-Ass Woman," and "Poem from the Mouth of God"; *H_NGM_N,* "Katie Condon, an American, One of the Roughs, a Kosmos in the Flesh"; *The Mackinac,* "Real Elegy," and "We Need to Talk"; *Indiana Review,* "Driving, 4 a.m."; *Narrative Magazine,* "Praying Naked," "Getting Through Monday," and "To the woman who accused me of not being a feminist, I'm sorry"; *Nashville Review,* "The Real Self Is Very Scary"; *New Ohio Review,* "Timestamps"; *The New Yorker,* "Origin"; *PUBLIC POOL,* "To Every Woman Who's Been Kept a Secret" and "Hymn"; *Tin House,* "Practicing Digressions" and "Parable"; *REALITY TUNNELS,* "Giving Myself Advice"; *Ruminate,* "At the #1 Fried Chicken & Seafood."

"The Sacrifice's Prayer" borrows the phrase "sea / at the back of my eyes" from Frank O'Hara's poem "In Memory of My Feelings."

"Katie Condon, an American, One of the Roughs, a Kosmos in the Flesh" borrows and slightly revises lines from Walt Whitman's *Leaves of Grass,* as well as a line from Vladimir Mayakovsky's *A Cloud in Trousers,* translated by John Glad and Daniel Weissbort.

With thanks to Sampson Starkweather for reading at Mongoose Vs. Cobra years ago, where I heard his line "I write / to become / historically / alone" from *La La La.* I use this line in "At Poetry Readings I'm Always Drunk."

In "I'm a Kick-Ass Woman" the phrase "as broad and innocent as a cabbage" is from Flannery O'Connor's short story "A Good Man is Hard to Find"; the line "This Is Just to Say" is the title of a William Carlos Williams poem; *"A Carafe Is a Blind / Ass"* plays on a line from Gertrude Stein's *Tender Buttons:* "A carafe is a blind glass."

The quoted line of Sappho in "Vow" is from Stephen Berg's translation of her poem "You Burn Me."

The refrain *"Senza tema di infamia ti rispondo"* in "At the #1 Chicken and Seafood" is from Dante's *Inferno.*

"The real self is very scary" is a line borrowed from Dorothea Lasky's poem "Whatever you paid for that sweater, it was worth it," which appears in her fantastic collection *AWE.*

I'm grateful to the University of Houston, the University of Tennessee, Inprint Houston, and the Bread Loaf Writer's Conference for the resources, instruction, and community that made this book possible. A special thank you to the University of Tennessee's College of Arts and Sciences for a fellowship that gave me the time to polish this collection. Thank you to Dawn Coleman and Bill Hardwig for use of the Director of Graduate Studies Discretionary Fund and for believing in these poems.

Heartfelt thanks to my teachers for their support in and beyond their classrooms: Kevin Prufer, Nick Flynn, Rebecca Gayle Howell, Ben Lee, Art Smith, Marilyn Kallet, Tom Cerasulo, Maria Stehle, and many others. Martha Serpas, thank you for the hours of soul-work, grief-work, and permission-giving during a dark time and in the years after. Joy Harjo, thank you for your continued lessons in intuition and trust. There is no space between here and there.

To those who read countless drafts of this book, especially Luci Brown, Jeb Herrin, Liam Hysjulien, Talia Mailman, David Tomas Martinez, Brynn Martin, Karyna McGlynn, Sam Mansfield, Bryan Owens, Jeremy Reed, Adam Walton, and Nicole Yackley, thank you for your insight and friendship. To Lindsey Alexander, Layla Benitez-James, Justin Boening and Devon Walker-Figueroa, Rachel Bracken, Tiana Clark, Allison Pitinii Davis, Steven Kleinman, Edgar Kunz, Nicole Laforet, Elysia Mann and Smudge the dog, Ellen Orner, and my fellow Bread Loaf waiters and staff: for the hours of poetry-talk that indirectly shaped this book, my endless gratitude.

Conor Bracken and Karissa Venne, you have combed over my poems more than anyone. Thank you for your generosity and care over the last decade.

Tony Hoagland: Thank you for being a shepherd to so many of these poems, and for your years of friendship. Save me a seat in the poetics course you're running in the ether.

Thank you to my family, especially my grandparents Ed and Carol Fedor for the endurance of their love; my parents and siblings-in-law for their enthusiasm and affection; my sister Meghan for being my first model of will, and for making beautiful art in her own right.

Mom and Dad, you said "yes" at all of the right times. As I am because of you, this book is because of you, and for you.

For believing in *Praying Naked,* Marcus Jackson, you have my deepest gratitude. Thank you to The Ohio State University Press, Mad Creek Books, and *The Journal.* My warmest thanks to Kristen Elias Rowley, Tara Cyphers, Laurie Avery, and Samara Rafert for their guidance.

To my husband, Richard: thank you for your steadfast belief in me and this book, and for your impeccable editorial eye. Thank you, most of all, for your love, which I return tenfold in this life and every life after.

And to you, reader: I'm so glad you're here.

The Journal Charles B. Wheeler Poetry Prize

Praying Naked
KATIE CONDON

Lethal Theater
SUSANNAH NEVISON

Radioapocrypha
BK FISCHER

June in Eden
ROSALIE MOFFETT

Somewhere in Space
TALVIKKI ANSEL

The River Won't Hold You
KARIN GOTTSHALL

Antidote
COREY VAN LANDINGHAM

Fair Copy
REBECCA HAZELTON

Blood Prism
EDWARD HAWORTH HOEPPNER

Men as Trees Walking
KEVIN HONOLD

American Husband
KARY WAYSON

Shadeland
ANDREW GRACE

Empire Burlesque
MARK SVENVOLD

Innocence
JEAN NORDHAUS

Autumn Road
BRIAN SWANN

Spot in the Dark
BETH GYLYS

Writing Letters for the Blind
GARY FINCKE

Mechanical Cluster
PATTY SEYBURN

Magical Thinking
JOSEPH DUEMER

Stone Sky Lifting
LIA PURPURA

Captivity Narrative
MARY ANN SAMYN

Blessings the Body Gave
WALT McDONALD

Anatomy, Errata
JUDITH HALL

Stones Don't Float: Poems Selected and New
JOHN HAAG

Crossing the Snow Bridge
FATIMA LIM-WILSON

The Creation
BRUCE BEASLEY

Night Thoughts and Henry Vaughan
DAVID YOUNG

History as a Second Language
DIONISIO D. MARTINEZ

Guests
TERESA CADER

Rooms, Which Were People
MARY CROSS

The Book of Winter
SUE OWEN

Life-list
ROBERT CORDING

Popular Culture
ALBERT GOLDBARTH